HOME PARTY (

35 COCKTAIL RECIPES EASY ENOUGH ᴛ∪ ᴀ

Emily Crossland

TABLE OF CONTENTS

AMERICANO

Known earlier as the Milano- Torino, for these were the two cities wherein its original ingredients were first made. Americano gives the most expensive bitter taste, which is perfect for a night party to be enjoyed with your loved ones.

INGREDIENTS

1 1/2 ounces Campari

1 1/2 ounces sweet vermouth

3 ounces chilled club soda

1 orange wheel and 1 lemon twist, for garnish

Plenty of ice

METHOD

Add enough ice into a rock glass and then add the Campari, sweet vermouth and club soda and stir well. Don't forget to chill the glass before making yourself this wonderful drink. As the final step, an orange wheel or a lemon twist on top of the glass will add an exquisite elegance to your delicious drink! Enjoy!

TIPS

You could substitute gin for the soda and enjoy the sumptuous taste.

BLOODY MARY

The cocktail with a name associated with some of the most influential women in ancient history such as Queen Mary I of England and Mary Pickford, the Hollywood actress, is a sumptuous cocktail and comes with a simple recipe!

INGREDIENTS

1 tablespoon celery salt (or plain kosher salt, if you prefer)

1/4 lemon, cut into two wedges

1/2 teaspoon Worcestershire sauce

1/4 teaspoon soy sauce

1/2 teaspoon freshly ground black pepper (or less to taste)

Dash of cayenne pepper

1/4 teaspoon hot sauce

1/2 teaspoon freshly grated horseradish (or 1 teaspoon prepared horseradish)

2 ounces vodka

4 ounces high-quality tomato juice

1 stick celery

METHOD

Put some celery salt onto a shallow dish, run a 12 ounce glass with the lemon wedge and dip it into the celery salt, fill it with ice and set aside.

Now take a cocktail shaker and add in the Worcestershire, soy, black pepper, cayenne pepper, hot sauce, and horseradish. Fill the shaker with enough ice and then add the vodka, tomato juice, and the remaining lemon juice.

Shake as hard as you can! Feel free to season as needed. Strain the mixture into the ice filled glass and garnish it with a celery stick and there it is! Buon Appetito!

TIPS

A perfect blend with grilled or fried shrimp, kebabs, sandwich wedges, fruit slices, and even sashimi!

Blue Hawaiian

Let your tastebuds enjoy the fruity splash of pineapple juice and all other delicious tropical flavours on a cold winter day, taking you to a hot sunny day at the deep blue sea! Make this simple recipe your favourite at your very own winter party.

Ingredients

50ml Bacardi Carta Blanca

50ml blue curaçao

1 teaspoon coconut cream

100ml pineapple juice

Method

It's too simple! Pour in all the ingredients into a cocktail shaker filled with lots of ice. Shake hard for 10 seconds and strain the drink into an ice-filled cocktail glass and serve! Cheers!

Tips

Replacing the rum with Vodka is certainly a wise choice and a delicious improvement that you must try out!

BOULEVARDIER

Despite many beliefs about the boulevardier being one of the variations of the Negroni, it has its own distinctive flavour and is sumptuous enough to remain unique. While the Negroni gives a crisp, light taste, the Boulevardier provides a rich and an intriguing satisfaction.

INGREDIENTS

1 ounce bourbon or rye whiskey

1 ounce Campari

1 ounce sweet vermouth

Garnish: orange twist or cherry

METHOD

All you have to do is combine the ingredients in a mixing glass filed with cracked ice. Stir well for 20 seconds and finally strain the mixture into a chilled cocktail glass. To give an added flavour, make sure to garnish your cocktail with a cherry or an orange peel.

TIPS

An amazing experience would be to add in Cynar in place of the vermouth or the Campari!

BROOKLYN

Being one of the five cocktails named for the boroughs of the New York city, Brooklyn provides a luscious pleasure to your tastebuds despite its rarity and what's more?! It has a simple recipe so you could enjoy its delicious sweetness right on your sofa!

INGREDIENTS

2 ounces rye or other whiskey

1 ounce dry vermouth

1/4 ounce maraschino liqueur

1/4 ounce Amer Picon, or a few dashes Angostura or orange bitters

METHOD

Grab a mixing glass and simply combine all the ingredients together, stir well for over 20 seconds with plenty of ice. All set! Strain the mixture into a chilled cocktail glass and enjoy!

TIPS

Getting bored with the Picon, don't worry, you can now spruce up your drink with Punt e Mes, Chartreuse or Cynar, as you wish!

Caipirinha

Made with Cachaça, this refreshing cocktail is Brazil's National cocktail, which you can now prepare right at your home for your own house party! The century old drink will delight you with a sophisticated sweet and strong flavour that is a must try!

Ingredients

1/2 ounce fresh lime juice, plus 3 lime wedges and 1 lime wheel

1 teaspoon sugar

1/2 ounce simple syrup

2 ounces cachaça

Method

Take a cocktail shaker filled with ice and add the lime juice, lime wedges, sugar and simple syrup and shake well. Now add the cachaça and another cup of ice and shake hard for about 30 seconds. It's time to taste! Pour the liquid into a rock glass and garnish your delicious cocktail with a lime wheel.

Tips

No cachaça? Don't worry! Add vodka in its place and you'll taste an improved caipirinha that is as tasty as the original drink!

CORPSE REVIVER

No, don't worry, this won't bring the dead back to living, in fact it sure will refresh and reinvigorate a whole party and what's more?! This is the perfect drink for a serious hangover.

INGREDIENTS

1 ounce gin

1/2 ounce Cointreau

1/2 ounce Lillet Blonde

3/4 ounce fresh lemon juice

Dash of Absinthe

METHOD

It's nothing complicated! Simply add in all the ingredients into a cocktail shaker, shake well for 15 seconds and strain it into a beautiful chilled cocktail glass! Bon Appétit!

TIPS

A perfect addition to this refreshing drink is half an ounce of simple syrup that will sweeten and refresh your tastebuds.

COSMOPOLITAN

A house party? This is undoubtedly the ideal cocktail that is a must in every party! Its origins dating back to the 1970s, the Cosmopolitan is the best Vodka sour anyone has ever made.

INGREDIENTS

1 1/2 ounces citrus-flavored vodka

1/2 ounce triple sec (Cointreau, preferably)

1/2 ounce cranberry juice

1/4 ounce lime juice (fresh, fresh, fresh only!)

Orange twist, for garnish

METHOD

Simple take a cocktail shaker, fill it with ice and add the vodka, triple sec, cranberry, and lime. Shake it vigorously for over 10 seconds and finally, strain it into a chilled cocktail glass.

For an extra added taste, don't forget to place an orange twist on the rim of the glass!

TIPS

If vodka and triple sec is not your ideal choice, you are more than free to replace them with orange juice and pink lemonade.

Daiquiri

The old-school daiquiri is simple yet adorns a unique simplicity and a taste that outruns all other cocktails and therefore is a must try at every household!

Ingredients

2 ounces light rum

3/4 ounce fresh-squeezed lime juice (about 1/2 of a lime)

1 teaspoon sugar

Method

Take a cocktail shaker and add lime juice and the sugar and stir well. Once all the sugar has fully dissolved, it is now time to add the rum and fill the shaker with ice and next, it's all about shaking! Shake for around 10 seconds and pour the content into a beautiful cocktail glass. Don't forget to add a lime wedge on the top of the glass.

Tips

You could really enjoy the daiquiri with half a banana or an avocado to enhance the relish.

French 75

The cocktail received its name after the French 75-mm field gun, used commonly in the World War I, and thus has a refreshing kick added to it with the gin, yet succeeds in stimulating the senses with its distinctive taste.

Ingredients

2 ounces gin

1 ounce freshly squeezed lemon juice

2 teaspoons sugar

Champagne or sparkling wine

Garnish: long thin lemon spiral and cocktail cherry

Method

It's all very simple! Take a cocktail shaker filled with ice. Add in the gin, lemon juice, and sugar and shake it well for over 15 seconds until it's fully chilled and that's it! Now pour the contents into a beautiful champagne flute.

To enjoy the absolute real taste, top the cocktail with champagne and stir gently. Finally take a long thin lemon spiral and a cocktail cherry to add elegance and flavour!

Tips

Some would much prefer their French 75 to include carbonated water replacing champagne, which would also be a pleasant alternative!

GIMLET

This classic cocktail was believed to have been named after Surgeon Admiral Sir Thomas Gimlette KCB and is the perfect gin sour that is not only perfect for an evening party but also to be enjoyed daily for more energy and refreshment!

INGREDIENTS

2 ounces gin

3/4 ounces lime cordial

Garnish: lime wedge

METHOD

Combine the ingredients in a mixing glass filled with ice. Stir well and strain it into a cocktail glass. Garnish with a lime wedge so you can satisfy your tastebuds with the best Gimlet cocktail ever!

TIPS

Many would also love to add simple syrup into this original cocktail which would be an amazing change to try out.

GIN FIZZ

Ready for the most hard shake you will ever have to make to get the perfect cocktail? Well, here it is! Gin Fizz is absolutely delicious only if you shake it well enough, but don't worry, it's alright to use the blender and it comes with an easy recipe! Great for a hot summer day, the Gin Fizz is the ideal for a morning breakfast or brunch.

INGREDIENTS

2 ounces gin

1 ounce cream

1 egg white

1/2 ounce lemon juice

1/2 ounce lime juice

2 teaspoons sugar, to taste

2-3 drops orange flower water

Seltzer

METHOD

First, combine everything except the seltzer in a cocktail shaker and you need to shake it for a maximum of 2 minutes without ice but you can also use a blender or a whisk if it's too hard, until there's enough foam being made. Then, it's time to add the ice and shake for another 20 seconds.

Finally strain the liquid into a Collins glass and add an ounce or two of cold Seltzer and that's it! Bon Appetite!

TIPS

Want to experience how the Japanese prefer their Gin Fizz? They add a bit of lychee liquor to the normal Gin Fizz and it is said to be amazingly delicious!

GODFATHER

This delicious blend of Scotch whisky and amaretto might seem simple but it promises to give you a sweet yet an extremely strong savour that is certain to delight all your tastebuds in a dash!

INGREDIENTS

1.5 ounce Scotch

1.5 ounce amaretto liqueur

Orange peel

METHOD

Add the Scotch and amaretto liqueur into a cocktail shaker and shake well for around 10 seconds. Add the ice and shake well once more. Pour this into an old fashioned glass and add the orange peel for garnishing and enjoy!

TIPS

Love bourbon?! Try adding bourbon into the Godfather instead of the scotch and yes! it does taste better!

Hanky Panky

"By Jove! That is the real hanky panky!" Very much like its mischievous name, this sweet and bitter drink will enhance your energy and spirits like no other!

Ingredients

50ml Gin

50ml Sweet Vermouth

5ml (or a couple of dashes) Fernet Branca

10ml freshly squeezed orange juice

Method

Put all the ingredients into a cocktail shaker and shake for around 20 seconds. Finally, strain the drink into a cocktail glass, and don't forget the orange peel for a better flavour! Cheers!

Tips

If you're too tired to shake, mixing together all the ingredients will not only make it easier and more faster but also give you an improved taste!

JackRose

The cocktail as many would say, is named after the infamous gambler Bald Jack Rose and is adorned with an exquisite combination of applejack and grenadine. The cocktail is sure to put you in an ecstatic pleasure that no other could ever provide.

Ingredients

2 ounces Laird's Applejack

3/4 ounce grenadine, preferably homemade

3/4 ounces fresh squeezed juice from 1 lemon

1 dash Peychaud's bitters

Lemon twist

Method

Nothing serious or complex, simply add the applejack, grenadine, lemon juice, and bitters into a cocktail shaker, fill the shaker with plenty of ice and shake it really well for a maximum of 15 seconds to get the complete, absolute savour. Once fully chilled, it's time to strain the cocktail into a martini glass.

Don't forget, squeeze some lemon juice over the surface of the drink and then run the lemon twist over the rim of the glass and enjoy!

Tips

You would be thrilled to taste the JackRose cocktail with some Irish Whiskey replacing the Applejack!

LAST WORD

The cocktail, that had gained popularity during the prohibition era and brought back to life by the local legend Murray Stenson, is a complex, herbaceous drink that would certainly leave any gin lover at a loss of words!

INGREDIENTS

3/4 ounce gin

3/4 ounce fresh-squeezed lime juice

3/4 ounce maraschino liqueur

3/4 ounce green Chartreuse

METHOD

It's so simple! All you have to do is combine all the ingredients in a cocktail shaker filled with ice and shake it hard for approximately 10 seconds. You can enjoy this appetizing cocktail in a chilled cocktail glass.

TIPS

It's a wonderful taste when you replace the gin with rye whiskey! Try and enjoy!

MARGARITA

Margarita, the Spanish word for "Daisy", is a breath-taking Mexican-American drink that is a must in every party!

INGREDIENTS

4 ounces tequila

2 ounces Cointreau

1 1/2 ounces fresh lime juice

Lime wedge, plus 2 lime wheels for garnish

1 tablespoon coarse salt, for glass rims

METHOD

Rock glasses are perfect for Margaritas, so take hold of two rock glasses and run the rim of each glass with the lime wedge and now dip them into the salt and set aside for the real magic to begin!

Grab a cocktail shaker and add the tequila, Cointreau, and the lime juice, fill it with ice and shake it for about 15 seconds until you see frost at the bottom of the shaker.

Finally, fill the ready-made glasses with ice and strain the margarita into each. Add a tasty twist to the cocktail by garnishing it with a lime wheel!

TIPS

Too bothered to shake it up? Don't worry, a great alternative is to serve it as a blended ice slush, and call it, 'frozen margarita'!

Mai Tai

It doesn't take a lot to say that this cocktail is good, its name itself spells it out for you! Mai tai is Italian for 'good', and not having enjoyed this is certainly a waste of life! The wonderful combination that it brings forth will give you a South Pacific summer day right at your home!

Ingredients

1 ½ parts Bacardi Carta Blanco

½ part Cointreau liqueur

¼ part lime juice

1 ½ parts pineapple juice

1 ½ parts orange juice

1 dash grenadine

1 part Bacardi Carta Negra

Cubed ice

To garnish: Lime wedge & mint

Method

Put the ingredients into a shaker with plenty of ice and shake for at least 20 seconds so that the liquid is chilled completely. Take a cocktail glass, fill it with ice and strain the liquid over the ice into the glass. The real added taste is when you place a lime wedge or a mint on the rim of the glass.

Tips

An extra zest of tequila into this tropical drink is sure to make the perfect Mai Tai into your favourite!

Manhattan

A classic cocktail renowned for being one of the six basic drinks listed in David A. Embury's classic *The Fine Art of Mixing Drinks* and is one of the most fashionable drinks in the cocktail world.

Ingredients

4 ounces rye whiskey

2 ounces sweet vermouth

4 dashes Angostura bitters

2 Maraschino cherries

Method

Take a mixing glass, fill it with ice and pour the whiskey, and the sweet vermouth. Add in the bitters for an extra and a unique taste of the real Manhattan! Now stir well until the shaker becomes too cold to touch on the outside, you could almost feel the taste!
Now take two cocktail glasses and place the cherries on each of them. Finally, divide the cocktail over the cherries and serve! Bon Appetite!

Tips

The cocktail is perfect with bourbon or Canadian whisky, which would become a splendid alternative to whiskey. A lemon peel may also serve as a sumptuous garnish!

MARTINI

The Martini Cocktail is certainly the king of all cocktails and the most elegant cocktail of them all, yet it remains the most iconic classic cocktail you could enjoy right at home.

INGREDIENTS

6 parts of Gin,

1 part of Dry Vermouth

Lemon twist

METHOD

Chill a martini glass, and top the mixing glass with abundant ice. Add the dry vermouth into this with a little stir so it would blend perfectly with the ice. Now, slowly add the gin and stir for another 15 seconds and don't forget to make sure the mixing glass is full to the brim with ice. That's it! Strain this into a beautiful martini glass and zest with a lemon peel to give the drink a twist! Enjoy!

TIPS

An olive twist would also add a perfect taste instead of the lemon peel.

MINT JULEP

A mint melting in your mouth is always an absolute refreshment and mint in a cocktail might just make your day! The taste of Southern United States, the Mint Julep is a splendid combination of bourbon and syrup blended with your favourite mint!

INGREDIENTS

2 teaspoons simple syrup

8 to 10 leaves fresh mint

Crushed ice

2 to 3 ounces bourbon, to taste

Mint sprigs, for garnish

METHOD

Add mint leaves and sugar syrup into a tall glass and slightly dissolve. Make sure not to overwork the mints or you'll miss out on the real taste! Next, fill the glass with ice up to half of the glass and add the bourbon. Fill the glass completely with ice and stir until you can see frost on the outside. If you think that's not enough ice, feel free to add more, and now for the best part! Sprinkle the fresh mint sprigs over the drink generously.
Serve the drink with a short straw so that the aromatic flavour of the mint will embrace the drinker with every single sip.

TIPS

Want to spice up your Mint Julep?! Add a ginger liqueur, such as Domaine de Canton, to add to the light and refreshing feeling of the cocktail.

MOJITO

This traditional Cuban cocktail is an excellent addition of sweetness to your sunny summer day! The sweet flavour of sugar blended with the rum and the soda will become the only thing you crave for some energy after a long sunny day.

INGREDIENTS

2 tablespoons (1 ounce) fresh lime juice

2 heaping teaspoons superfine sugar

1 cup crushed ice

12 fresh mint leaves, plus 5 small sprigs for garnish

1/4 cup (2 ounces) white rum

2 tablespoons (1 ounce) club soda

METHOD

Mix lime juice and sugar in a tall glass such as a Collins glass. Once the sugar has dissolved completely, add 1/4 cup of crushed ice.
Run some mint leaves over the rim of the glass for the aromatic flavour and add the rest into the drink. Stir lightly for over 15 seconds and then add rum, remaining crushed ice, and the club soda. Gently stir for another 5 seconds. As the last step, lace some mint sprigs on the rim, insert a tall straw and Cheers!

TIPS

If you think the Mojito's too sweet, don't worry you're not the only one to think so, add some Angostura bitters to cut the sweetness and spice up the drink.

NEGRONI

With a blend of both sweet and bitter and the refreshing herbal flavour, it's hard not to like the negroni cocktail! This iconic Italian drink is a must try for all cocktail lovers!

INGREDIENTS

1 ounce dry gin

1 ounce Campari

1 ounce sweet vermouth

Orange peel

METHOD

It is important to remember that you can serve a Negroni in two ways:
1. If you wish to serve it on the rocks, all you have to do is to mix all the ingredients in a classic glass with plenty of ice, stir well and place a twist of orange peel on the rim for both aroma and taste
2. Serving Negroni straight up is also a splendid idea and all it takes is to stir all the ingredients in an ice-filled mixing glass for around 20 seconds and finally pour the content into a chilled cocktail glass. Don't forget to add the orange peel for extra taste and aroma!

TIPS

You could also replace the gin with sparkling white wine, or Prosecco for a greater variation and a blasting change!

OLD CUBAN

Introduced in 2004, the Caribbean drink is extra-refreshing with a blend of fresh mint, rum and some fizz. Want to impress your friends at the party?! check this out!

INGREDIENTS

45ml rum, such as Bacardi 8

30ml lime juice

30ml sugar syrup

8 mint leaves

1 dash Angostura Bitters

Cubed ice

A mint leaf to garnish

METHOD

Squish the lime juice, syrup and mint using a muddler or a rolling pin in a cocktail shaker. Now add the rum, ice and the angostura bitters. Shake well for about 20 seconds and strain it into a cocktail glass. Don't forget to garnish with a mint leaf to experience the refreshing delish!

TIPS

Top the drink with champagne to get the complete real taste of the Old Cuban.

Old Fashioned

What better way to drink a simple sour whiskey! The perfect drink to catch up with your old friends and family with this combination of sour, sweet, spicy and aromatic cocktail.

Ingredients

1 sugar cube

3 dashes Angostura bitters

2 ounces bourbon

1 tablespoon club soda

1 thin strip of lemon peel

Method

Take a rock glass and add in the sugar cube, bitters and club soda. Muddle well until a paste has formed. It's time to add the bourbon and ice and shake well for the last time. Enjoy your drink with a strip of lemon peel for an extra chill!

Tips

Try replacing the whiskey with the brandy and you won't regret it!

PALOMA

Wonder what a mix of tequila and grapefruit would taste like? It's none other than a Paloma! You can now try out Mexico's most beloved cocktail right at you own home bar, sipping on your sofa with your friends and family!

INGREDIENTS

Kosher salt

1 grapefruit wedge

¼ cup fresh grapefruit juice

1 tablespoon fresh lime juice

1 teaspoon sugar

¼ cup mescal or tequila

¼ cup club soda

METHOD

Put a little kosher salt on a plate and run half of the rim of a highball glass on the salt and rub the grapefruit wedge on the other half of the glass. Add in the grapefruit juice, lime juice, and sugar into the glass and stir well until the sugar is well dissolved. Now pour the mescal, more ice and finish off with soda. Finally, for the real absolute taste, garnish with a grapefruit wedge!

TIPS

If you think the drink lacks a sense of bitterness, you can add a dash of Campari to kick some bitterness into the drink.

Pisco Sour

For all those sour lovers, there's nothing more delicious and divine than the Pisco Sour cocktail! In fact, the drink is so ionic that Peru celebrates a National Pisco Sour Day and did you know that there's a Pisco Sour Festival in Lima?!

Ingredients

3 ounces Pisco

1 ounce fresh-squeezed lime juice

3/4 ounce simple syrup

1 fresh egg white

1 dash Angostura or Amargo bitters

Method

First, add Pisco, lime, simple syrup, and egg white in a cocktail shaker and seal it tight without adding any ice. Shake hard for over 10 seconds until you see foams in the egg whites. It's time to add the ice and start shaking hard for another 10 seconds until thoroughly chilled. You're done! Strain the drink into a cocktail glass and don't forget to dash some bitters atop the egg white foam!

Tips

As many Bolivians would love, you could replace the lime juice with orange juice for anyone who prefers oranges over lime!

PLANTER'S PUNCH

Is it a golden summer day outside?! Then the Planter's Punch is the perfect cocktail for the day! It's cold and delightful with a blend of full-flavored rum with lime juice, sugar, some form of spice and plenty of ice that is sure to give you a blasting refreshment.

INGREDIENTS

3 ounces Coruba dark Jamaican rum (if you can't find Coruba, substitute another dark, heavy rum)

1 ounce simple syrup (equal parts sugar and water, mixed until dissolved)

3/4 ounce fresh lime juice

3 dashes Angostura bitters

A mint sprig

METHOD

Fill a tall glass with crushed ice and add all the ingredients into it. Now swizzle with a bar spoon until you can see frost forming on the outside. All set! Add some more ice and garnish with a mint sprig for a better revitalizing feeling.

TIPS

You could also add pineapple juice or orange juice to sour up or sweeten your cocktail as you wish!

Rob Roy

Imagine adding scotch into a Manhattan cocktail. That's what the Rob Roy would give you! Created in the New York City and named after an operetta, this sweet flavoured drink is the ideal cocktail for any summer party!

Ingredients

2 ½ ounce Blended Scotch

1 ounce Sweet Vermouth

2 dashes of Angostura

2 maraschino cherries or a lemon twist for garnish

Method

Fill the mixing glass with ice and combine all the ingredients except the garnishes. Stir well to mix for around 20 seconds. That's it! Now pour the drink into chilled rock glasses, top it with more ice and place the cherries or the lemon twist on the rim.

Tips

Feel free to add a dash of Angostura bitters to enhance the colour and the bitterness.

SCREWDRIVER

Despite its name, the splendid blend of vodka and orange juice is the absolute drink for a beautiful summer day. You may wonder how the delicious cocktail got its name, actually in the old days, the drink was made by stirring with a screwdriver! But don't worry, you can still use the spoon and get the most elegant screwdriver cocktail at home!

INGREDIENTS

1 1/2 fluid ounces vodka

6 fluid ounces orange juice

1 1/2 cups ice cubes

METHOD

Choose a nice elegant highball glass, put in the vodka and the orange juice, stir well to combine and finally, add ice before tasting!

TIPS

Adding Galliano to your cocktail would become an excellent combination to the original Screwdriver cocktail and it's a must try!

Side Car

A cousin of the Margarita family, and while a Margarita is perfect for a sunny, warm day, the side car is a perfect suit for a cold night by a fire due to its light, mellow taste.

Ingredients

2 ounces VSOP Cognac, Armagnac, or good California brandy

1 ounce Cointreau

3/4 ounce fresh lemon juice

Superfine sugar, for garnish (optional)

Method

Put the brandy, Cointreau, and the lemon juice into a cocktail shaker and fill with ice. Shake the shaker! Shake well for about 10 seconds until it has chilled completely.

It's time to prepare the glass. Run a lemon wedge over the rim of the cocktail glass and then dip it into fine sugar so that it makes a thin crust on the rim, chill the glass as required and strain the cocktail into the glass and enjoy!

Tips

A wonderful variation is to add pineapple juice into the mixture making a summer version of your favourite side car!

Tom Collins

The perfect cocktail for a perfect sunny day! Dating its origins back to more than a century and a half, this delicious blend of gin and sparkling lemonade drink gives a most refreshing crispiness, that will keep your energy high all day!

Ingredients

2 ounces gin

Juice of 1/2 a lemon

1 teaspoon sugar (preferably superfine)

Chilled club soda

Method

Combine the gin, lemon and sugar in a Collins glass and stir until all the sugar has finely dissolved. Next, fill the glass with lots of ice and top it with chilled club soda! Insert a straw and you're already in heaven!

Tips

Instead of the sugar, don't hesitate to use simple syrup to make the process even more easier!

WHISKEY SOUR

In a night party and looking for a basic light cocktail? Try out the Whiskey Sour! This adds a splendid sour taste with a blend of bourbon and lemon juice, and the perfect suit for a pleasant evening after a long tired day.

INGREDIENTS

2 ounces whiskey

1 ounce fresh-squeezed lemon juice

1 teaspoon sugar

1 egg white (optional)

METHOD

All it takes for you is to simply grab a cocktail shaker, add in all the ingredients, fill it with ice and start shaking for over 10 seconds.
Remember, if you decide to use the egg white, you might have to shake a little harder for a little more than 10 seconds.
You can select between a chilled cocktail glass or even an ice filled old fashioned glass to strain the drink and don't forget to place a cherry, or an orange slice to refresh your tastebuds. Cheers!

TIPS

You are free to change the base spirit of the recipe with a different sour flavour, such as Amaretto Sour, Apricot Sour, Brandy Sour or Gin Sour.

WHITE RUSSIAN

This creamy coffee flavoured cocktail with a dose of vodka is a favourite for all coffee lovers. While you enjoy sipping this delish right at your sofa, remember, although there isn't any Russian origin to this drink, its name comes from the vodka that is added, which enhances its real taste.

INGREDIENTS

2 fluid ounces vodka

1 fluid ounce coffee-flavored liqueur

1 fluid ounce heavy cream

1 cup ice

2 drops of vanilla extract

METHOD

Choose an old fashioned glass to give an authentic hue to the drink! Add the vodka, coffee liqueur, vanilla extract and ice into it and stir well. Finally, add the cream (you could even add milk) and stir once more. Cheers to a rich and creamy delight!

TIPS

For some, cream might seem boring, but there's a splendid substitute! Add Baileys Irish Cream to enrich the taste and offer a whole new experience!

ZOMBIE

Feel the intensity you'd feel if you saw a real zombie with a simple drink! A simple combination of apricot brandy, lime, and pineapple juice will not only spice up your party but also add some fire and light into it.

INGREDIENTS

1 1/2 ounces amber rum

1/2 ounce dark rum

1/2 ounce 151-proof rum

3/4 ounce fresh pineapple juice

3/4 ounce fresh lime juice

1/2 ounce Velvet Falernum

1/2 ounce brown sugar simple syrup (brown sugar dissolved in equal part simmering water and cooled)

Mint sprig, for garnish

METHOD

First, fill your cocktail shaker with lots of ice and then add all the liquids. It's time to shake! Shake for around 30 seconds and finally, pour the drink into an ice-filled tiki mug. Add the mint sprig on the rim for a complete delicacy!

TIPS

Adding a dash of grapefruit juice to this delicious beverage will enrich your brunch at a small tiki party!

ONE LAST THING...

If you enjoyed this book or found it useful I'd be very grateful if you'd post a short review on a website you bought it from. Your support really does make a difference and I read all the reviews personally so I can get your feedback and make this book even better.

Thanks again for your support!

Printed in Great Britain
by Amazon